Introduction

After over a decade working as a dieti
body image coach, I've learned that w
looking to build better habits, reframe unhelpful thought
patterns, or accomplish big goals, their transition from where
they are to where they want to be often starts with a simple
check-in.

That's why I created The Daily Check-In Journal: a tool to tune
into your body, mind, and heart, acknowledge moments
throughout your day that might otherwise go unnoticed, and
gain clarity on where you could use more support.

Use this journal consistently - daily or even multiple times per
day - as a tool to feel more grounded, focused, and connected.
Be gentle with yourself if you skip a day, week, or even a
month. The pages are undated so you can come back to the
practice of checking in whenever you feel called.

Ultimately, this journal can be used whatever way suits you
best. Start and end each day with the prompts, or use the
journal as a prompt itself to check-in throughout the day and
answer a prompt here and there. You can skip any prompts
that don't resonate on any given day, or even create your own
prompts in the "free write" sections.

The key to these prompts is to take them at face value. Try not
to pathologize or psychoanalyze your sensations, feelings, or
thoughts. The prompts are simply a practice for tuning in,
noticing, and acknowledging. And while there are no right or
wrong answers, I've offered some more detailed instructions
for how to use each prompt on the following pages.

Happy Journaling,

Jessi

The Prompts

What feedback am I receiving from my body right now?
The feedback we receive from our body can easily go unnoticed when we're not checking in. While this is not an exhaustive list of body sensations, It can be helpful to think about checking in with these three systems for the sake of this prompt:

- **Musculoskeletal Systems:** This can include any pain, soreness, or aches in your muscles and joints. Or alternatively, comfort, looseness, or overall sense of ease in the body.

- **Physiological Systems:** This can include your hunger, thirst, breathing, heart rate, temperature (warm, cold, neutral), bladder fullness, or sex drive.

- **Nervous Systems:** This can include changes in heart rate or breathing but might also include those hard-to-name sensations like butterflies or a pit in your stomach, tightness in the chest area, or an overall sense of tension in the body.

If possible, be specific with the sensations you are experiencing. For example, if you're feeling hungry, you might want to note if it's a subtle hunger or extreme hunger. Tuning into these sensations takes practice, so be patient with yourself if this doesn't come easy.

What feelings or emotions am I experiencing right now?
Naming emotions can be challenging because we are often feeling more than one emotion at any given time. If you're having difficulty naming emotions, see if any of the words below resonate, but keep in mind this is not an exhaustive list (you can also search "feeling wheels" for a more comprehensive list). And remember, you don't have to try to "fix" the feeling. Simply notice the feeling, and acknowledge the feeling by writing it down.

Happy	Anxious	Sadness	Angry
Content	Overwhelm	Grief	Bored
Joy	Fear	Loneliness	Rage
Excited	Scared	Guilt	Frustrated
Confident	Vulnerable	Shame	Confused
Grounded	Stressed	Despair	Annoyed
Playful	Confused	Apathetic	Envious

The Prompts

What am I craving today?

I purposefully put this question here so you could use the information you just gathered to (potentially) inform what you're craving. This could be something general like food, rest, movement, or social connection. Or, you can get really specific and list a specific food you're craving, a song you want to listen to, or a specific activity you'd like to incorporate into your day. Try to be honest about what you are craving, not what you think you should be craving. Some of these things might be realistic and some might be dreams. Either way, write it down.

What's on my mind?

This prompt is for those nagging thoughts thats we just can't shake. It might be something you're worrying about or something you just need to get off your chest. Use this as an opportunity to get those thoughts out of your head and onto paper.

What can I do to support myself today? What do I need?

Now, a more tangible question. What kind of support do you need today? Is there anything you can do to support yourself? Is there someone you can reach out to to ask for support? This might look like packing snacks to bring to work or asking for help in taking a task or project off your plate.

My intention for the day is...

This prompt is intended to be more about how you want to approach your day, versus what you want to accomplish today. For example: My intention for the day is...

- To honor my craving for connection by reaching out to a friend.
- To respect my body's desire for rest by taking frequent breaks.
- To approach my relationships with curiosity and playfulness.

The PM Prompts

These evening prompts are more straight forward and direct. They are designed to be more reflective where as the morning questions are more "of the moment". Use these prompts as a way to capture the wins, identify the challenges, and lock in your favorite memories.

You're ready to start your Daily Check-In practice! Happy Journaling!

AM CHECK-IN

What feedback am I receiving from my body right now?
Pain, hunger, fullness warmth, cold, butterflies in stomach, etc.

_____

_____

_____

_____

What feelings or emotions am I experiencing right now?
Sadness, anger, grief, happiness, excitement, worry, anxiety etc.

_____

_____

_____

_____

What am I craving today?
This could be a specific food, or something more general like comfort, or connection.

_____

_____

_____

_____

What's on my mind?
What can't I stop thinking about? What do I need to get off my chest?

_____

_____

_____

_____

What can I do to support myself today? What do I need?

_____

_____

_____

_____

My intention for the day is...

_____

_____

_____

_____

PM CHECK-IN

What went well today?

_____

_____

_____

What did I find challenging today?

_____

_____

_____

What's a win (no matter how small) worth celebrating today?

_____

_____

_____

A moment I want to remember from today:

_____

_____

_____

FREE WRITE

_____

_____

_____

_____

_____

_____

_____

AM CHECK-IN

What feedback am I receiving from my body right now?
Pain, hunger, fullness warmth, cold, butterflies in stomach, etc.

_____

_____

_____

_____

What feelings or emotions am I experiencing right now?
Sadness, anger, grief, happiness, excitement, worry, anxiety etc.

_____

_____

_____

_____

What am I craving today?
This could be a specific food, or something more general like comfort, or connection.

_____

_____

_____

_____

What's on my mind?
What can't I stop thinking about? What do I need to get off my chest?

_____

_____

_____

_____

What can I do to support myself today? What do I need?

_____

_____

_____

_____

My intention for the day is...

_____

_____

_____

PM CHECK-IN

What went well today?

_____

_____

_____

What did I find challenging today?

_____

_____

_____

What's a win (no matter how small) worth celebrating today?

_____

_____

_____

A moment I want to remember from today:

_____

_____

_____

FREE WRITE

_____

_____

_____

_____

_____

_____

_____

_____

AM CHECK-IN

What feedback am I receiving from my body right now?
Pain, hunger, fullness warmth, cold, butterflies in stomach, etc.

_____

_____

_____

_____

What feelings or emotions am I experiencing right now?
Sadness, anger, grief, happiness, excitement, worry, anxiety etc.

_____

_____

_____

_____

What am I craving today?
This could be a specific food, or something more general like comfort, or connection.

_____

_____

_____

_____

What's on my mind?
What can't I stop thinking about? What do I need to get off my chest?

_____

_____

_____

_____

What can I do to support myself today? What do I need?

_____

_____

_____

_____

My intention for the day is...

_____

_____

_____

_____

PM CHECK-IN

What went well today?

_____

_____

_____

_____

What did I find challenging today?

_____

_____

_____

_____

What's a win (no matter how small) worth celebrating today?

_____

_____

_____

_____

A moment I want to remember from today:

_____

_____

_____

_____

FREE WRITE

_____

_____

_____

_____

_____

_____

_____

_____

_____

AM CHECK-IN

What feedback am I receiving from my body right now?
Pain, hunger, fullness warmth, cold, butterflies in stomach, etc.

_____

_____

_____

_____

What feelings or emotions am I experiencing right now?
Sadness, anger, grief, happiness, excitement, worry, anxiety etc.

_____

_____

_____

_____

What am I craving today?
This could be a specific food, or something more general like comfort, or connection.

_____

_____

_____

_____

What's on my mind?
What can't I stop thinking about? What do I need to get off my chest?

_____

_____

_____

_____

What can I do to support myself today? What do I need?

_____

_____

_____

_____

My intention for the day is...

_____

_____

_____

PM CHECK-IN

What went well today?

_____

_____

_____

_____

What did I find challenging today?

_____

_____

_____

_____

What's a win (no matter how small) worth celebrating today?

_____

_____

_____

_____

A moment I want to remember from today:

_____

_____

_____

_____

FREE WRITE

_____

_____

_____

_____

_____

_____

_____

_____

_____

AM CHECK-IN

Date: _____

What feedback am I receiving from my body right now?
Pain, hunger, fullness warmth, cold, butterflies in stomach, etc.

_____

_____

_____

_____

What feelings or emotions am I experiencing right now?
Sadness, anger, grief, happiness, excitement, worry, anxiety etc.

_____

_____

_____

_____

What am I craving today?
This could be a specific food, or something more general like comfort, or connection.

_____

_____

_____

_____

What's on my mind?
What can't I stop thinking about? What do I need to get off my chest?

_____

_____

_____

_____

What can I do to support myself today? What do I need?

_____

_____

_____

_____

My intention for the day is...

_____

_____

_____

_____

PM CHECK-IN

What went well today?

_____

_____

_____

What did I find challenging today?

_____

_____

_____

What's a win (no matter how small) worth celebrating today?

_____

_____

_____

A moment I want to remember from today:

_____

_____

_____

_____

FREE WRITE

_____

_____

_____

_____

_____

_____

_____

_____

AM CHECK-IN

What feedback am I receiving from my body right now?
Pain, hunger, fullness warmth, cold, butterflies in stomach, etc.

_____

_____

_____

_____

What feelings or emotions am I experiencing right now?
Sadness, anger, grief, happiness, excitement, worry, anxiety etc.

_____

_____

_____

_____

What am I craving today?
This could be a specific food, or something more general like comfort, or connection.

_____

_____

_____

_____

What's on my mind?
What can't I stop thinking about? What do I need to get off my chest?

_____

_____

_____

_____

What can I do to support myself today? What do I need?

_____

_____

_____

_____

My intention for the day is...

_____

_____

_____

_____

PM CHECK-IN

What went well today?

_____

_____

_____

_____

What did I find challenging today?

_____

_____

_____

_____

What's a win (no matter how small) worth celebrating today?

_____

_____

_____

_____

A moment I want to remember from today:

_____

_____

_____

_____

FREE WRITE

_____

_____

_____

_____

_____

_____

_____

_____

_____

AM CHECK-IN

What feedback am I receiving from my body right now?
Pain, hunger, fullness warmth, cold, butterflies in stomach, etc.

_____

_____

_____

_____

What feelings or emotions am I experiencing right now?
Sadness, anger, grief, happiness, excitement, worry, anxiety etc.

_____

_____

_____

_____

What am I craving today?
This could be a specific food, or something more general like comfort, or connection.

_____

_____

_____

_____

What's on my mind?
What can't I stop thinking about? What do I need to get off my chest?

_____

_____

_____

_____

What can I do to support myself today? What do I need?

_____

_____

_____

_____

My intention for the day is...

_____

_____

_____

PM CHECK-IN

What went well today?

_____

_____

_____

_____

What did I find challenging today?

_____

_____

_____

_____

What's a win (no matter how small) worth celebrating today?

_____

_____

_____

_____

A moment I want to remember from today:

_____

_____

_____

_____

FREE WRITE

_____

_____

_____

_____

_____

_____

_____

_____

_____

AM CHECK-IN

What feedback am I receiving from my body right now?
Pain, hunger, fullness warmth, cold, butterflies in stomach, etc.

_____

_____

_____

_____

What feelings or emotions am I experiencing right now?
Sadness, anger, grief, happiness, excitement, worry, anxiety etc.

_____

_____

_____

_____

What am I craving today?
This could be a specific food, or something more general like comfort, or connection.

_____

_____

_____

_____

What's on my mind?
What can't I stop thinking about? What do I need to get off my chest?

_____

_____

_____

_____

What can I do to support myself today? What do I need?

_____

_____

_____

_____

My intention for the day is...

_____

_____

_____

_____

PM CHECK-IN

What went well today?

_____
_____
_____

What did I find challenging today?

_____
_____
_____

What's a win (no matter how small) worth celebrating today?

_____
_____
_____

A moment I want to remember from today:

_____
_____
_____

FREE WRITE

_____
_____
_____
_____
_____
_____
_____
_____

AM CHECK-IN

What feedback am I receiving from my body right now?
Pain, hunger, fullness warmth, cold, butterflies in stomach, etc.

_____

_____

_____

_____

What feelings or emotions am I experiencing right now?
Sadness, anger, grief, happiness, excitement, worry, anxiety etc.

_____

_____

_____

_____

What am I craving today?
This could be a specific food, or something more general like comfort, or connection.

_____

_____

_____

_____

What's on my mind?
What can't I stop thinking about? What do I need to get off my chest?

_____

_____

_____

_____

What can I do to support myself today? What do I need?

_____

_____

_____

_____

My intention for the day is...

_____

_____

_____

_____

PM CHECK-IN

What went well today?

_____

_____

_____

_____

What did I find challenging today?

_____

_____

_____

_____

What's a win (no matter how small) worth celebrating today?

_____

_____

_____

_____

A moment I want to remember from today:

_____

_____

_____

_____

FREE WRITE

_____

_____

_____

_____

_____

_____

_____

_____

AM CHECK-IN

Date: _____

What feedback am I receiving from my body right now?
Pain, hunger, fullness warmth, cold, butterflies in stomach, etc.

_____

_____

_____

_____

What feelings or emotions am I experiencing right now?
Sadness, anger, grief, happiness, excitement, worry, anxiety etc.

_____

_____

_____

_____

What am I craving today?
This could be a specific food, or something more general like comfort, or connection.

_____

_____

_____

_____

What's on my mind?
What can't I stop thinking about? What do I need to get off my chest?

_____

_____

_____

_____

What can I do to support myself today? What do I need?

_____

_____

_____

_____

My intention for the day is...

_____

_____

_____

PM CHECK-IN

What went well today?

_____
_____
_____

What did I find challenging today?

_____
_____
_____

What's a win (no matter how small) worth celebrating today?

_____
_____
_____

A moment I want to remember from today:

_____
_____
_____

FREE WRITE

_____
_____
_____
_____
_____
_____
_____

AM CHECK-IN

What feedback am I receiving from my body right now?
Pain, hunger, fullness warmth, cold, butterflies in stomach, etc.

_____

_____

_____

_____

What feelings or emotions am I experiencing right now?
Sadness, anger, grief, happiness, excitement, worry, anxiety etc.

_____

_____

_____

_____

What am I craving today?
This could be a specific food, or something more general like comfort, or connection.

_____

_____

_____

_____

What's on my mind?
What can't I stop thinking about? What do I need to get off my chest?

_____

_____

_____

_____

What can I do to support myself today? What do I need?

_____

_____

_____

_____

My intention for the day is...

_____

_____

_____

_____

PM CHECK-IN

What went well today?

_____

_____

_____

What did I find challenging today?

_____

_____

_____

What's a win (no matter how small) worth celebrating today?

_____

_____

_____

A moment I want to remember from today:

_____

_____

_____

FREE WRITE

_____

_____

_____

_____

_____

_____

_____

_____

Date: _____

AM CHECK-IN

What feedback am I receiving from my body right now?
Pain, hunger, fullness warmth, cold, butterflies in stomach, etc.

_____

_____

_____

_____

What feelings or emotions am I experiencing right now?
Sadness, anger, grief, happiness, excitement, worry, anxiety etc.

_____

_____

_____

_____

What am I craving today?
This could be a specific food, or something more general like comfort, or connection.

_____

_____

_____

_____

What's on my mind?
What can't I stop thinking about? What do I need to get off my chest?

_____

_____

_____

_____

What can I do to support myself today? What do I need?

_____

_____

_____

_____

My intention for the day is...

_____

_____

_____

_____

PM CHECK-IN

What went well today?

_____

_____

_____

_____

What did I find challenging today?

_____

_____

_____

_____

What's a win (no matter how small) worth celebrating today?

_____

_____

_____

_____

A moment I want to remember from today:

_____

_____

_____

_____

FREE WRITE

_____

_____

_____

_____

_____

_____

_____

_____

_____

AM CHECK-IN

What feedback am I receiving from my body right now?
Pain, hunger, fullness warmth, cold, butterflies in stomach, etc.

_____

_____

_____

_____

What feelings or emotions am I experiencing right now?
Sadness, anger, grief, happiness, excitement, worry, anxiety etc.

_____

_____

_____

_____

What am I craving today?
This could be a specific food, or something more general like comfort, or connection.

_____

_____

_____

_____

What's on my mind?
What can't I stop thinking about? What do I need to get off my chest?

_____

_____

_____

_____

What can I do to support myself today? What do I need?

_____

_____

_____

_____

My intention for the day is...

_____

_____

_____

PM CHECK-IN

What went well today?

_____

_____

_____

What did I find challenging today?

_____

_____

_____

What's a win (no matter how small) worth celebrating today?

_____

_____

_____

A moment I want to remember from today:

_____

_____

_____

FREE WRITE

_____

_____

_____

_____

_____

_____

_____

AM CHECK-IN

Date: _____

What feedback am I receiving from my body right now?
Pain, hunger, fullness warmth, cold, butterflies in stomach, etc.

_____

_____

_____

_____

What feelings or emotions am I experiencing right now?
Sadness, anger, grief, happiness, excitement, worry, anxiety etc.

_____

_____

_____

_____

What am I craving today?
This could be a specific food, or something more general like comfort, or connection.

_____

_____

_____

_____

What's on my mind?
What can't I stop thinking about? What do I need to get off my chest?

_____

_____

_____

_____

What can I do to support myself today? What do I need?

_____

_____

_____

_____

My intention for the day is...

_____

_____

_____

_____

PM CHECK-IN

What went well today?

_____

_____

_____

What did I find challenging today?

_____

_____

_____

What's a win (no matter how small) worth celebrating today?

_____

_____

_____

A moment I want to remember from today:

_____

_____

_____

FREE WRITE

_____

_____

_____

_____

_____

_____

_____

_____

Date: _____

AM CHECK-IN

What feedback am I receiving from my body right now?
Pain, hunger, fullness warmth, cold, butterflies in stomach, etc.

_____

_____

_____

_____

What feelings or emotions am I experiencing right now?
Sadness, anger, grief, happiness, excitement, worry, anxiety etc.

_____

_____

_____

_____

What am I craving today?
This could be a specific food, or something more general like comfort, or connection.

_____

_____

_____

_____

What's on my mind?
What can't I stop thinking about? What do I need to get off my chest?

_____

_____

_____

_____

What can I do to support myself today? What do I need?

_____

_____

_____

_____

My intention for the day is...

_____

_____

_____

PM CHECK-IN

What went well today?

_____

_____

_____

_____

What did I find challenging today?

_____

_____

_____

_____

What's a win (no matter how small) worth celebrating today?

_____

_____

_____

_____

A moment I want to remember from today:

_____

_____

_____

_____

FREE WRITE

_____

_____

_____

_____

_____

_____

_____

_____

Date: _____

AM CHECK-IN

What feedback am I receiving from my body right now?
Pain, hunger, fullness warmth, cold, butterflies in stomach, etc.

_____

_____

_____

_____

What feelings or emotions am I experiencing right now?
Sadness, anger, grief, happiness, excitement, worry, anxiety etc.

_____

_____

_____

_____

What am I craving today?
This could be a specific food, or something more general like comfort, or connection.

_____

_____

_____

_____

What's on my mind?
What can't I stop thinking about? What do I need to get off my chest?

_____

_____

_____

_____

What can I do to support myself today? What do I need?

_____

_____

_____

_____

My intention for the day is...

_____

_____

_____

_____

PM CHECK-IN

What went well today?

_____

_____

_____

_____

What did I find challenging today?

_____

_____

_____

_____

What's a win (no matter how small) worth celebrating today?

_____

_____

_____

_____

A moment I want to remember from today:

_____

_____

_____

_____

FREE WRITE

_____

_____

_____

_____

_____

_____

_____

_____

AM CHECK-IN

What feedback am I receiving from my body right now?
Pain, hunger, fullness warmth, cold, butterflies in stomach, etc.

_____

_____

_____

_____

What feelings or emotions am I experiencing right now?
Sadness, anger, grief, happiness, excitement, worry, anxiety etc.

_____

_____

_____

_____

What am I craving today?
This could be a specific food, or something more general like comfort, or connection.

_____

_____

_____

_____

What's on my mind?
What can't I stop thinking about? What do I need to get off my chest?

_____

_____

_____

_____

What can I do to support myself today? What do I need?

_____

_____

_____

_____

My intention for the day is...

_____

_____

_____

_____

PM CHECK-IN

What went well today?

_____
_____
_____
_____

What did I find challenging today?

_____
_____
_____
_____

What's a win (no matter how small) worth celebrating today?

_____
_____
_____
_____

A moment I want to remember from today:

_____
_____
_____
_____

FREE WRITE

_____
_____
_____
_____
_____
_____
_____
_____

AM CHECK-IN

What feedback am I receiving from my body right now?
Pain, hunger, fullness warmth, cold, butterflies in stomach, etc.

_____

_____

_____

_____

What feelings or emotions am I experiencing right now?
Sadness, anger, grief, happiness, excitement, worry, anxiety etc.

_____

_____

_____

_____

What am I craving today?
This could be a specific food, or something more general like comfort, or connection.

_____

_____

_____

_____

What's on my mind?
What can't I stop thinking about? What do I need to get off my chest?

_____

_____

_____

_____

What can I do to support myself today? What do I need?

_____

_____

_____

_____

My intention for the day is...

_____

_____

_____

_____

PM CHECK-IN

What went well today?

_____

_____

_____

What did I find challenging today?

_____

_____

_____

What's a win (no matter how small) worth celebrating today?

_____

_____

_____

A moment I want to remember from today:

_____

_____

_____

FREE WRITE

_____

_____

_____

_____

_____

_____

_____

_____

AM CHECK-IN

Date: _____

What feedback am I receiving from my body right now?
Pain, hunger, fullness warmth, cold, butterflies in stomach, etc.

_____
_____
_____
_____

What feelings or emotions am I experiencing right now?
Sadness, anger, grief, happiness, excitement, worry, anxiety etc.

_____
_____
_____
_____

What am I craving today?
This could be a specific food, or something more general like comfort, or connection.

_____
_____
_____
_____

What's on my mind?
What can't I stop thinking about? What do I need to get off my chest?

_____
_____
_____
_____

What can I do to support myself today? What do I need?

_____
_____
_____
_____

My intention for the day is...

_____
_____
_____
_____

PM CHECK-IN

What went well today?

_____

_____

_____

_____

What did I find challenging today?

_____

_____

_____

_____

What's a win (no matter how small) worth celebrating today?

_____

_____

_____

_____

A moment I want to remember from today:

_____

_____

_____

_____

FREE WRITE

_____

_____

_____

_____

_____

_____

_____

_____

AM CHECK-IN

What feedback am I receiving from my body right now?
Pain, hunger, fullness warmth, cold, butterflies in stomach, etc.

_____

_____

_____

_____

What feelings or emotions am I experiencing right now?
Sadness, anger, grief, happiness, excitement, worry, anxiety etc.

_____

_____

_____

_____

What am I craving today?
This could be a specific food, or something more general like comfort, or connection.

_____

_____

_____

_____

What's on my mind?
What can't I stop thinking about? What do I need to get off my chest?

_____

_____

_____

_____

What can I do to support myself today? What do I need?

_____

_____

_____

_____

My intention for the day is...

_____

_____

_____

_____

PM CHECK-IN

What went well today?

_____
_____
_____
_____

What did I find challenging today?

_____
_____
_____
_____

What's a win (no matter how small) worth celebrating today?

_____
_____
_____
_____

A moment I want to remember from today:

_____
_____
_____
_____

FREE WRITE

_____
_____
_____
_____
_____
_____
_____
_____

AM CHECK-IN

What feedback am I receiving from my body right now?
Pain, hunger, fullness warmth, cold, butterflies in stomach, etc.

_____

_____

_____

_____

What feelings or emotions am I experiencing right now?
Sadness, anger, grief, happiness, excitement, worry, anxiety etc.

_____

_____

_____

_____

What am I craving today?
This could be a specific food, or something more general like comfort, or connection.

_____

_____

_____

_____

What's on my mind?
What can't I stop thinking about? What do I need to get off my chest?

_____

_____

_____

_____

What can I do to support myself today? What do I need?

_____

_____

_____

_____

My intention for the day is...

_____

_____

_____

_____

PM CHECK-IN

What went well today?

_____
_____
_____

What did I find challenging today?

_____
_____
_____

What's a win (no matter how small) worth celebrating today?

_____
_____
_____

A moment I want to remember from today:

_____
_____
_____

FREE WRITE

_____
_____
_____
_____
_____
_____
_____

AM CHECK-IN

Date: _____

What feedback am I receiving from my body right now?
Pain, hunger, fullness warmth, cold, butterflies in stomach, etc.

_____

_____

_____

_____

What feelings or emotions am I experiencing right now?
Sadness, anger, grief, happiness, excitement, worry, anxiety etc.

_____

_____

_____

_____

What am I craving today?
This could be a specific food, or something more general like comfort, or connection.

_____

_____

_____

_____

What's on my mind?
What can't I stop thinking about? What do I need to get off my chest?

_____

_____

_____

_____

What can I do to support myself today? What do I need?

_____

_____

_____

_____

My intention for the day is...

_____

_____

_____

PM CHECK-IN

What went well today?

_____

_____

_____

_____

What did I find challenging today?

_____

_____

_____

_____

What's a win (no matter how small) worth celebrating today?

_____

_____

_____

_____

A moment I want to remember from today:

_____

_____

_____

_____

FREE WRITE

_____

_____

_____

_____

_____

_____

_____

_____

AM CHECK-IN

What feedback am I receiving from my body right now?
Pain, hunger, fullness warmth, cold, butterflies in stomach, etc.

_____

_____

_____

_____

What feelings or emotions am I experiencing right now?
Sadness, anger, grief, happiness, excitement, worry, anxiety etc.

_____

_____

_____

_____

What am I craving today?
This could be a specific food, or something more general like comfort, or connection.

_____

_____

_____

_____

What's on my mind?
What can't I stop thinking about? What do I need to get off my chest?

_____

_____

_____

_____

What can I do to support myself today? What do I need?

_____

_____

_____

_____

My intention for the day is...

_____

_____

_____

_____

PM CHECK-IN

What went well today?

_____

_____

_____

What did I find challenging today?

_____

_____

_____

What's a win (no matter how small) worth celebrating today?

_____

_____

_____

A moment I want to remember from today:

_____

_____

_____

FREE WRITE

_____

_____

_____

_____

_____

_____

_____

AM CHECK-IN

What feedback am I receiving from my body right now?
Pain, hunger, fullness warmth, cold, butterflies in stomach, etc.

_____

_____

_____

_____

What feelings or emotions am I experiencing right now?
Sadness, anger, grief, happiness, excitement, worry, anxiety etc.

_____

_____

_____

_____

What am I craving today?
This could be a specific food, or something more general like comfort, or connection.

_____

_____

_____

_____

What's on my mind?
What can't I stop thinking about? What do I need to get off my chest?

_____

_____

_____

_____

What can I do to support myself today? What do I need?

_____

_____

_____

_____

My intention for the day is...

_____

_____

_____

_____

PM CHECK-IN

What went well today?

_____

_____

_____

What did I find challenging today?

_____

_____

_____

What's a win (no matter how small) worth celebrating today?

_____

_____

_____

A moment I want to remember from today:

_____

_____

_____

FREE WRITE

_____

_____

_____

_____

_____

_____

_____

_____

AM CHECK-IN

Date: _____

What feedback am I receiving from my body right now?
Pain, hunger, fullness warmth, cold, butterflies in stomach, etc.

_____

_____

_____

_____

What feelings or emotions am I experiencing right now?
Sadness, anger, grief, happiness, excitement, worry, anxiety etc.

_____

_____

_____

_____

What am I craving today?
This could be a specific food, or something more general like comfort, or connection.

_____

_____

_____

_____

What's on my mind?
What can't I stop thinking about? What do I need to get off my chest?

_____

_____

_____

_____

What can I do to support myself today? What do I need?

_____

_____

_____

_____

My intention for the day is...

_____

_____

_____

_____

PM CHECK-IN

What went well today?

_____

_____

_____

What did I find challenging today?

_____

_____

_____

What's a win (no matter how small) worth celebrating today?

_____

_____

_____

A moment I want to remember from today:

_____

_____

_____

FREE WRITE

_____

_____

_____

_____

_____

_____

_____

_____

AM CHECK-IN

What feedback am I receiving from my body right now?
Pain, hunger, fullness warmth, cold, butterflies in stomach, etc.

_____

_____

_____

_____

What feelings or emotions am I experiencing right now?
Sadness, anger, grief, happiness, excitement, worry, anxiety etc.

_____

_____

_____

_____

What am I craving today?
This could be a specific food, or something more general like comfort, or connection.

_____

_____

_____

_____

What's on my mind?
What can't I stop thinking about? What do I need to get off my chest?

_____

_____

_____

_____

What can I do to support myself today? What do I need?

_____

_____

_____

_____

My intention for the day is...

_____

_____

_____

_____

PM CHECK-IN

What went well today?

_____
_____
_____

What did I find challenging today?

_____
_____
_____

What's a win (no matter how small) worth celebrating today?

_____
_____
_____

A moment I want to remember from today:

_____
_____
_____

FREE WRITE

_____
_____
_____
_____
_____
_____
_____
_____

Date: _____

AM CHECK-IN

What feedback am I receiving from my body right now?
Pain, hunger, fullness warmth, cold, butterflies in stomach, etc.

_____

_____

_____

_____

What feelings or emotions am I experiencing right now?
Sadness, anger, grief, happiness, excitement, worry, anxiety etc.

_____

_____

_____

_____

What am I craving today?
This could be a specific food, or something more general like comfort, or connection.

_____

_____

_____

_____

What's on my mind?
What can't I stop thinking about? What do I need to get off my chest?

_____

_____

_____

_____

What can I do to support myself today? What do I need?

_____

_____

_____

_____

My intention for the day is...

_____

_____

_____

PM CHECK-IN

What went well today?

_____
_____
_____
_____

What did I find challenging today?

_____
_____
_____
_____

What's a win (no matter how small) worth celebrating today?

_____
_____
_____
_____

A moment I want to remember from today:

_____
_____
_____
_____

FREE WRITE

_____
_____
_____
_____
_____
_____
_____
_____

AM CHECK-IN

What feedback am I receiving from my body right now?
Pain, hunger, fullness warmth, cold, butterflies in stomach, etc.

_____

_____

_____

_____

What feelings or emotions am I experiencing right now?
Sadness, anger, grief, happiness, excitement, worry, anxiety etc.

_____

_____

_____

_____

What am I craving today?
This could be a specific food, or something more general like comfort, or connection.

_____

_____

_____

_____

What's on my mind?
What can't I stop thinking about? What do I need to get off my chest?

_____

_____

_____

_____

What can I do to support myself today? What do I need?

_____

_____

_____

_____

My intention for the day is...

_____

_____

_____

_____

PM CHECK-IN

What went well today?

_____
_____
_____
_____

What did I find challenging today?

_____
_____
_____
_____

What's a win (no matter how small) worth celebrating today?

_____
_____
_____
_____

A moment I want to remember from today:

_____
_____
_____
_____

FREE WRITE

_____
_____
_____
_____
_____
_____
_____
_____

Date: _____

AM CHECK-IN

What feedback am I receiving from my body right now?
Pain, hunger, fullness warmth, cold, butterflies in stomach, etc.

_____

_____

_____

_____

What feelings or emotions am I experiencing right now?
Sadness, anger, grief, happiness, excitement, worry, anxiety etc.

_____

_____

_____

_____

What am I craving today?
This could be a specific food, or something more general like comfort, or connection.

_____

_____

_____

_____

What's on my mind?
What can't I stop thinking about? What do I need to get off my chest?

_____

_____

_____

_____

What can I do to support myself today? What do I need?

_____

_____

_____

_____

My intention for the day is...

_____

_____

_____

_____

PM CHECK-IN

What went well today?

_____

_____

_____

What did I find challenging today?

_____

_____

_____

What's a win (no matter how small) worth celebrating today?

_____

_____

_____

A moment I want to remember from today:

_____

_____

_____

FREE WRITE

_____

_____

_____

_____

_____

_____

_____

_____

AM CHECK-IN

What feedback am I receiving from my body right now?
Pain, hunger, fullness warmth, cold, butterflies in stomach, etc.

_____

_____

_____

_____

What feelings or emotions am I experiencing right now?
Sadness, anger, grief, happiness, excitement, worry, anxiety etc.

_____

_____

_____

_____

What am I craving today?
This could be a specific food, or something more general like comfort, or connection.

_____

_____

_____

_____

What's on my mind?
What can't I stop thinking about? What do I need to get off my chest?

_____

_____

_____

_____

What can I do to support myself today? What do I need?

_____

_____

_____

_____

My intention for the day is...

_____

_____

_____

_____

PM CHECK-IN

What went well today?

_____
_____
_____

What did I find challenging today?

_____
_____
_____

What's a win (no matter how small) worth celebrating today?

_____
_____
_____

A moment I want to remember from today:

_____
_____
_____

FREE WRITE

_____
_____
_____
_____
_____
_____
_____

Date: _____

AM CHECK-IN

What feedback am I receiving from my body right now?
Pain, hunger, fullness warmth, cold, butterflies in stomach, etc.

_____
_____
_____
_____

What feelings or emotions am I experiencing right now?
Sadness, anger, grief, happiness, excitement, worry, anxiety etc.

_____
_____
_____
_____

What am I craving today?
This could be a specific food, or something more general like comfort, or connection.

_____
_____
_____
_____

What's on my mind?
What can't I stop thinking about? What do I need to get off my chest?

_____
_____
_____
_____

What can I do to support myself today? What do I need?

_____
_____
_____
_____

My intention for the day is...

_____
_____
_____

PM CHECK-IN

What went well today?

_____

_____

_____

What did I find challenging today?

_____

_____

_____

What's a win (no matter how small) worth celebrating today?

_____

_____

_____

A moment I want to remember from today:

_____

_____

_____

FREE WRITE

_____

_____

_____

_____

_____

_____

_____

_____

Date: _____

AM CHECK-IN

What feedback am I receiving from my body right now?
Pain, hunger, fullness warmth, cold, butterflies in stomach, etc.

_____

_____

_____

_____

What feelings or emotions am I experiencing right now?
Sadness, anger, grief, happiness, excitement, worry, anxiety etc.

_____

_____

_____

_____

What am I craving today?
This could be a specific food, or something more general like comfort, or connection.

_____

_____

_____

_____

What's on my mind?
What can't I stop thinking about? What do I need to get off my chest?

_____

_____

_____

_____

What can I do to support myself today? What do I need?

_____

_____

_____

_____

My intention for the day is...

_____

_____

_____

_____

PM CHECK-IN

What went well today?

_____

_____

_____

_____

What did I find challenging today?

_____

_____

_____

_____

What's a win (no matter how small) worth celebrating today?

_____

_____

_____

_____

A moment I want to remember from today:

_____

_____

_____

_____

FREE WRITE

_____

_____

_____

_____

_____

_____

_____

_____

_____

AM CHECK-IN

What feedback am I receiving from my body right now?
Pain, hunger, fullness warmth, cold, butterflies in stomach, etc.

_____

_____

_____

_____

What feelings or emotions am I experiencing right now?
Sadness, anger, grief, happiness, excitement, worry, anxiety etc.

_____

_____

_____

_____

What am I craving today?
This could be a specific food, or something more general like comfort, or connection.

_____

_____

_____

_____

What's on my mind?
What can't I stop thinking about? What do I need to get off my chest?

_____

_____

_____

_____

What can I do to support myself today? What do I need?

_____

_____

_____

_____

My intention for the day is...

_____

_____

_____

_____

PM CHECK-IN

What went well today?

_____

_____

_____

_____

What did I find challenging today?

_____

_____

_____

What's a win (no matter how small) worth celebrating today?

_____

_____

_____

_____

A moment I want to remember from today:

_____

_____

_____

_____

FREE WRITE

_____

_____

_____

_____

_____

_____

_____

_____

AM CHECK-IN

What feedback am I receiving from my body right now?
Pain, hunger, fullness warmth, cold, butterflies in stomach, etc.

_____

_____

_____

_____

What feelings or emotions am I experiencing right now?
Sadness, anger, grief, happiness, excitement, worry, anxiety etc.

_____

_____

_____

_____

What am I craving today?
This could be a specific food, or something more general like comfort, or connection.

_____

_____

_____

_____

What's on my mind?
What can't I stop thinking about? What do I need to get off my chest?

_____

_____

_____

_____

What can I do to support myself today? What do I need?

_____

_____

_____

_____

My intention for the day is...

_____

_____

_____

_____

PM CHECK-IN

What went well today?

_____

_____

_____

_____

What did I find challenging today?

_____

_____

_____

_____

What's a win (no matter how small) worth celebrating today?

_____

_____

_____

_____

A moment I want to remember from today:

_____

_____

_____

_____

FREE WRITE

_____

_____

_____

_____

_____

_____

_____

_____

AM CHECK-IN

What feedback am I receiving from my body right now?
Pain, hunger, fullness warmth, cold, butterflies in stomach, etc.

_____

_____

_____

_____

What feelings or emotions am I experiencing right now?
Sadness, anger, grief, happiness, excitement, worry, anxiety etc.

_____

_____

_____

_____

What am I craving today?
This could be a specific food, or something more general like comfort, or connection.

_____

_____

_____

_____

What's on my mind?
What can't I stop thinking about? What do I need to get off my chest?

_____

_____

_____

_____

What can I do to support myself today? What do I need?

_____

_____

_____

_____

My intention for the day is...

_____

_____

_____

_____

PM CHECK-IN

What went well today?

_____

_____

_____

What did I find challenging today?

_____

_____

_____

What's a win (no matter how small) worth celebrating today?

_____

_____

_____

A moment I want to remember from today:

_____

_____

_____

FREE WRITE

_____

_____

_____

_____

_____

_____

_____

_____

Date: _____

AM CHECK-IN

What feedback am I receiving from my body right now?
Pain, hunger, fullness warmth, cold, butterflies in stomach, etc.

_____

_____

_____

_____

What feelings or emotions am I experiencing right now?
Sadness, anger, grief, happiness, excitement, worry, anxiety etc.

_____

_____

_____

_____

What am I craving today?
This could be a specific food, or something more general like comfort, or connection.

_____

_____

_____

_____

What's on my mind?
What can't I stop thinking about? What do I need to get off my chest?

_____

_____

_____

_____

What can I do to support myself today? What do I need?

_____

_____

_____

_____

My intention for the day is...

_____

_____

_____

_____

PM CHECK-IN

What went well today?

_____

_____

_____

What did I find challenging today?

_____

_____

_____

What's a win (no matter how small) worth celebrating today?

_____

_____

_____

A moment I want to remember from today:

_____

_____

_____

FREE WRITE

_____

_____

_____

_____

_____

_____

_____

Date: _____

AM CHECK-IN

What feedback am I receiving from my body right now?
Pain, hunger, fullness warmth, cold, butterflies in stomach, etc.

_____

_____

_____

_____

What feelings or emotions am I experiencing right now?
Sadness, anger, grief, happiness, excitement, worry, anxiety etc.

_____

_____

_____

_____

What am I craving today?
This could be a specific food, or something more general like comfort, or connection.

_____

_____

_____

_____

What's on my mind?
What can't I stop thinking about? What do I need to get off my chest?

_____

_____

_____

_____

What can I do to support myself today? What do I need?

_____

_____

_____

_____

My intention for the day is...

_____

_____

_____

_____

PM CHECK-IN

What went well today?

_____

_____

_____

_____

What did I find challenging today?

_____

_____

_____

_____

What's a win (no matter how small) worth celebrating today?

_____

_____

_____

_____

A moment I want to remember from today:

_____

_____

_____

_____

FREE WRITE

_____

_____

_____

_____

_____

_____

_____

_____

AM CHECK-IN

What feedback am I receiving from my body right now?
Pain, hunger, fullness warmth, cold, butterflies in stomach, etc.

_____

_____

_____

_____

What feelings or emotions am I experiencing right now?
Sadness, anger, grief, happiness, excitement, worry, anxiety etc.

_____

_____

_____

_____

What am I craving today?
This could be a specific food, or something more general like comfort, or connection.

_____

_____

_____

_____

What's on my mind?
What can't I stop thinking about? What do I need to get off my chest?

_____

_____

_____

_____

What can I do to support myself today? What do I need?

_____

_____

_____

_____

My intention for the day is...

_____

_____

_____

_____

PM CHECK-IN

What went well today?

_____
_____
_____

What did I find challenging today?

_____
_____
_____

What's a win (no matter how small) worth celebrating today?

_____
_____
_____

A moment I want to remember from today:

_____
_____
_____

FREE WRITE

_____
_____
_____
_____
_____
_____
_____

AM CHECK-IN

What feedback am I receiving from my body right now?
Pain, hunger, fullness warmth, cold, butterflies in stomach, etc.

_____

_____

_____

_____

What feelings or emotions am I experiencing right now?
Sadness, anger, grief, happiness, excitement, worry, anxiety etc.

_____

_____

_____

_____

What am I craving today?
This could be a specific food, or something more general like comfort, or connection.

_____

_____

_____

_____

What's on my mind?
What can't I stop thinking about? What do I need to get off my chest?

_____

_____

_____

_____

What can I do to support myself today? What do I need?

_____

_____

_____

_____

My intention for the day is...

_____

_____

_____

_____

PM CHECK-IN

What went well today?

_____

_____

_____

What did I find challenging today?

_____

_____

_____

What's a win (no matter how small) worth celebrating today?

_____

_____

_____

A moment I want to remember from today:

_____

_____

_____

FREE WRITE

_____

_____

_____

_____

_____

_____

_____

_____

AM CHECK-IN

What feedback am I receiving from my body right now?
Pain, hunger, fullness warmth, cold, butterflies in stomach, etc.

_____

_____

_____

_____

What feelings or emotions am I experiencing right now?
Sadness, anger, grief, happiness, excitement, worry, anxiety etc.

_____

_____

_____

_____

What am I craving today?
This could be a specific food, or something more general like comfort, or connection.

_____

_____

_____

_____

What's on my mind?
What can't I stop thinking about? What do I need to get off my chest?

_____

_____

_____

_____

What can I do to support myself today? What do I need?

_____

_____

_____

_____

My intention for the day is...

_____

_____

_____

_____

PM CHECK-IN

What went well today?

_____
_____
_____
_____

What did I find challenging today?

_____
_____
_____
_____

What's a win (no matter how small) worth celebrating today?

_____
_____
_____
_____

A moment I want to remember from today:

_____
_____
_____
_____

FREE WRITE

_____
_____
_____
_____
_____
_____
_____
_____

AM CHECK-IN

What feedback am I receiving from my body right now?
Pain, hunger, fullness warmth, cold, butterflies in stomach, etc.

_____

_____

_____

_____

What feelings or emotions am I experiencing right now?
Sadness, anger, grief, happiness, excitement, worry, anxiety etc.

_____

_____

_____

_____

What am I craving today?
This could be a specific food, or something more general like comfort, or connection.

_____

_____

_____

_____

What's on my mind?
What can't I stop thinking about? What do I need to get off my chest?

_____

_____

_____

_____

What can I do to support myself today? What do I need?

_____

_____

_____

_____

My intention for the day is...

_____

_____

_____

_____

PM CHECK-IN

What went well today?

_____

_____

_____

What did I find challenging today?

_____

_____

_____

What's a win (no matter how small) worth celebrating today?

_____

_____

_____

A moment I want to remember from today:

_____

_____

_____

FREE WRITE

_____

_____

_____

_____

_____

_____

_____

_____

AM CHECK-IN

Date: _____

What feedback am I receiving from my body right now?
Pain, hunger, fullness warmth, cold, butterflies in stomach, etc.

_____

_____

_____

_____

What feelings or emotions am I experiencing right now?
Sadness, anger, grief, happiness, excitement, worry, anxiety etc.

_____

_____

_____

_____

What am I craving today?
This could be a specific food, or something more general like comfort, or connection.

_____

_____

_____

_____

What's on my mind?
What can't I stop thinking about? What do I need to get off my chest?

_____

_____

_____

_____

What can I do to support myself today? What do I need?

_____

_____

_____

_____

My intention for the day is...

_____

_____

_____

_____

PM CHECK-IN

What went well today?

_____

_____

_____

_____

What did I find challenging today?

_____

_____

_____

_____

What's a win (no matter how small) worth celebrating today?

_____

_____

_____

_____

A moment I want to remember from today:

_____

_____

_____

_____

FREE WRITE

_____

_____

_____

_____

_____

_____

_____

_____

AM CHECK-IN

What feedback am I receiving from my body right now?
Pain, hunger, fullness warmth, cold, butterflies in stomach, etc.

_____

_____

_____

_____

What feelings or emotions am I experiencing right now?
Sadness, anger, grief, happiness, excitement, worry, anxiety etc.

_____

_____

_____

_____

What am I craving today?
This could be a specific food, or something more general like comfort, or connection.

_____

_____

_____

_____

What's on my mind?
What can't I stop thinking about? What do I need to get off my chest?

_____

_____

_____

_____

What can I do to support myself today? What do I need?

_____

_____

_____

_____

My intention for the day is...

_____

_____

_____

_____

PM CHECK-IN

What went well today?

_____
_____
_____
_____

What did I find challenging today?

_____
_____
_____
_____

What's a win (no matter how small) worth celebrating today?

_____
_____
_____
_____

A moment I want to remember from today:

_____
_____
_____
_____

FREE WRITE

_____
_____
_____
_____
_____
_____
_____
_____

AM CHECK-IN

Date: _____

What feedback am I receiving from my body right now?
Pain, hunger, fullness warmth, cold, butterflies in stomach, etc.

_____

_____

_____

_____

What feelings or emotions am I experiencing right now?
Sadness, anger, grief, happiness, excitement, worry, anxiety etc.

_____

_____

_____

_____

What am I craving today?
This could be a specific food, or something more general like comfort, or connection.

_____

_____

_____

_____

What's on my mind?
What can't I stop thinking about? What do I need to get off my chest?

_____

_____

_____

_____

What can I do to support myself today? What do I need?

_____

_____

_____

_____

My intention for the day is...

_____

_____

_____

_____

PM CHECK-IN

What went well today?

_____

_____

_____

_____

What did I find challenging today?

_____

_____

_____

_____

What's a win (no matter how small) worth celebrating today?

_____

_____

_____

_____

A moment I want to remember from today:

_____

_____

_____

_____

FREE WRITE

_____

_____

_____

_____

_____

_____

_____

_____

Date: _____

AM CHECK-IN

What feedback am I receiving from my body right now?
Pain, hunger, fullness warmth, cold, butterflies in stomach, etc.

_____

_____

_____

_____

What feelings or emotions am I experiencing right now?
Sadness, anger, grief, happiness, excitement, worry, anxiety etc.

_____

_____

_____

_____

What am I craving today?
This could be a specific food, or something more general like comfort, or connection.

_____

_____

_____

_____

What's on my mind?
What can't I stop thinking about? What do I need to get off my chest?

_____

_____

_____

_____

What can I do to support myself today? What do I need?

_____

_____

_____

_____

My intention for the day is...

_____

_____

_____

_____

PM CHECK-IN

What went well today?

_____

_____

_____

_____

What did I find challenging today?

_____

_____

_____

_____

What's a win (no matter how small) worth celebrating today?

_____

_____

_____

_____

A moment I want to remember from today:

_____

_____

_____

_____

FREE WRITE

_____

_____

_____

_____

_____

_____

_____

_____

AM CHECK-IN

What feedback am I receiving from my body right now?
Pain, hunger, fullness warmth, cold, butterflies in stomach, etc.

_____

_____

_____

_____

What feelings or emotions am I experiencing right now?
Sadness, anger, grief, happiness, excitement, worry, anxiety etc.

_____

_____

_____

_____

What am I craving today?
This could be a specific food, or something more general like comfort, or connection.

_____

_____

_____

_____

What's on my mind?
What can't I stop thinking about? What do I need to get off my chest?

_____

_____

_____

_____

What can I do to support myself today? What do I need?

_____

_____

_____

_____

My intention for the day is...

_____

_____

_____

_____

PM CHECK-IN

What went well today?

_____

_____

_____

What did I find challenging today?

_____

_____

_____

What's a win (no matter how small) worth celebrating today?

_____

_____

_____

A moment I want to remember from today:

_____

_____

_____

FREE WRITE

_____

_____

_____

_____

_____

_____

_____

_____

Date: _____

AM CHECK-IN

What feedback am I receiving from my body right now?
Pain, hunger, fullness warmth, cold, butterflies in stomach, etc.

_____

_____

_____

_____

What feelings or emotions am I experiencing right now?
Sadness, anger, grief, happiness, excitement, worry, anxiety etc.

_____

_____

_____

_____

What am I craving today?
This could be a specific food, or something more general like comfort, or connection.

_____

_____

_____

_____

What's on my mind?
What can't I stop thinking about? What do I need to get off my chest?

_____

_____

_____

_____

What can I do to support myself today? What do I need?

_____

_____

_____

_____

My intention for the day is...

_____

_____

_____

_____

PM CHECK-IN

What went well today?

_____
_____
_____
_____

What did I find challenging today?

_____
_____
_____
_____

What's a win (no matter how small) worth celebrating today?

_____
_____
_____
_____

A moment I want to remember from today:

_____
_____
_____
_____

FREE WRITE

_____
_____
_____
_____
_____
_____
_____
_____

AM CHECK-IN

What feedback am I receiving from my body right now?
Pain, hunger, fullness warmth, cold, butterflies in stomach, etc.

_____

_____

_____

_____

What feelings or emotions am I experiencing right now?
Sadness, anger, grief, happiness, excitement, worry, anxiety etc.

_____

_____

_____

_____

What am I craving today?
This could be a specific food, or something more general like comfort, or connection.

_____

_____

_____

_____

What's on my mind?
What can't I stop thinking about? What do I need to get off my chest?

_____

_____

_____

_____

What can I do to support myself today? What do I need?

_____

_____

_____

_____

My intention for the day is...

_____

_____

_____

_____

PM CHECK-IN

What went well today?

_____
_____
_____
_____

What did I find challenging today?

_____
_____
_____
_____

What's a win (no matter how small) worth celebrating today?

_____
_____
_____
_____

A moment I want to remember from today:

_____
_____
_____
_____

FREE WRITE

_____
_____
_____
_____
_____
_____
_____
_____

About the Author

Jessi Haggerty is a Registered Dietitian, Certified Intuitive Eating Counselor, and Certified Personal Trainer. She received her Bachelors of Science in Nutrition and Dietetics from Boston University and completed her Dietetic Internship at Oregon Health and Science University.

Today, Jessi has a private practice based just outside of Boston, Massachusetts and specializes in helping her clients improve their relationship with food and their bodies so they can show up for what matters most in their life. Jessi is a Health at Every Size® practitioner, focusing on intuitive eating and movement, eating disorder recovery and weight inclusive medical nutrition therapy.

You can learn more subscribe to her weekly newsletter for more journaling prompts at www.JessiHaggerty.com or connect with her on Instagram at @JessiHaggertyRD.

Made in the USA
Monee, IL
08 July 2025

20715450R00056